BUILDING BLOCKS OF GEOGRAPHY

ATMOSPHERE AND WEATHER

Written by Alex Woolf

Illustrated by Steve Evans

WORLD BOOK

a Scott Fetzer company
Chicago

World Book, Inc.
180 North LaSalle Street
Suite 900
Chicago, Illinois 60601
USA

For information about other World Book publications, visit our website at www.worldbook.com or call 1-800-WORLDBK (967-5325).
For information about sales to schools and libraries, call 1-800-975-3250 (United States), or 1-800-837-5365 (Canada).

© 2023 World Book, Inc. All rights reserved. This volume may not be reproduced in whole or in part in any form without prior written permission from the publisher.

WORLD BOOK and the GLOBE DEVICE are registered trademarks or trademarks of World Book, Inc.

Library of Congress Cataloging-in-Publication Data for this volume has been applied for.

Building Blocks of Geography
ISBN: 978-0-7166-4275-6 (set, hc.)

Atmosphere and Weather
ISBN: 978-0-7166-4276-3 (hc.)

Also available as:
ISBN: 978-0-7166-4286-2 (e-book)

Printed in India by Thomson Press (India) Limited, Uttar Pradesh, India
3rd printing November 2024

WORLD BOOK STAFF
Executive Committee
President: Geoff Broderick
Vice President, Editorial: Tom Evans
Vice President, Finance: Donald D. Keller
Vice President, Marketing: Jean Lin
Vice President, International: Eddy Kisman
Vice President, Technology: Jason Dole
Director, Human Resources: Bev Ecker

Editorial
Manager, New Content: Jeff De La Rosa
Associate Manager, New Product: Nicholas Kilzer
Sr. Editor: Shawn Brennan
Proofreader: Nathalie Strassheim

Graphics and Design
Sr. Visual Communications Designer: Melanie Bender
Sr. Web Designer/Digital Media Developer: Matt Carrington
Coordinator, Design Development: Brenda Tropinski

Acknowledgments:
Writer: Alex Woolf
Illustrator: Steve Evans
Series advisor: Marjorie Frank

Developed with World Book by White-Thomson Publishing LTD
www.wtpub.co.uk

Additional spot art by Shutterstock

TABLE OF CONTENTS

What is the Atmosphere? 4
The Layers of the Atmosphere 8
The Weather 10
Air Temperature 14
Air Pressure 18
Humidity 22
Clouds 24
Wind 26
Prevailing Winds 28
Air Masses 30
Fronts 32
Extreme Weather 34
Looking After the Atmosphere 36
Activity: Weather or Not! 38
Words to Know 40

There is a glossary on page 40. Terms defined in the glossary are in type **that looks like this** on their first appearance.

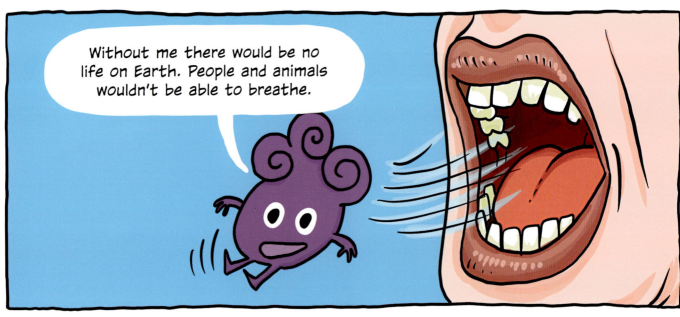

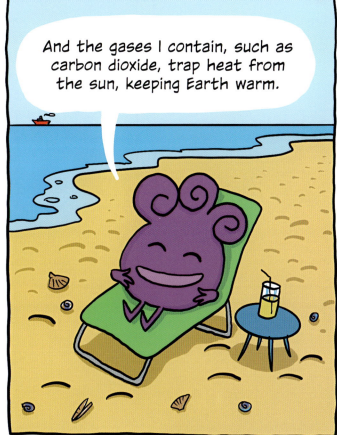

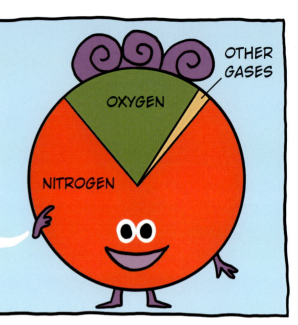

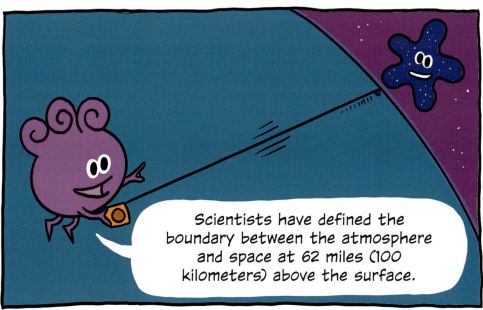

THE LAYERS OF THE ATMOSPHERE

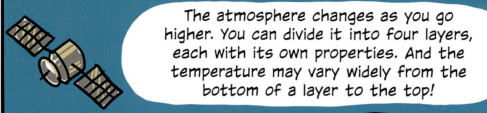

The atmosphere changes as you go higher. You can divide it into four layers, each with its own properties. And the temperature may vary widely from the bottom of a layer to the top!

Height: 50 miles (80 kilometers)

The lowest temperatures in the atmosphere occur in the third layer, the **mesosphere.** Above the poles, summer temperatures can fall below -200 °F (-130 °C). The air in the mesosphere is too thin for airplanes and balloons to fly there.

Height: about 30 miles (48 kilometers)

The second lowest layer, the **stratosphere,** contains around 80 to 90 percent of the atmosphere's ozone (a gas that blocks harmful rays from the sun, protecting life on Earth). The stratosphere is nearly cloudless and extremely dry. In the polar regions, ice clouds form during winter.

Height: about 12 miles (19 kilometers) above the equator and 6 miles (10 kilometers) above the poles.

THERMOSPHERE   Average temperature: about -130 °F (-90 °C)

The uppermost layer, the **thermosphere,** extends all the way into space. The air in the thermosphere is extremely thin and changes in composition the higher you go. Above about 600 miles (1000 kilometers), the thermosphere contains mainly hydrogen and helium.

 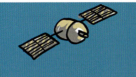

Average temperature: over 2000 °F (1000 °C) at about 200 miles (300 kilometers)

Average temperature: -130 °F (-90 °C)

MESOSPHERE

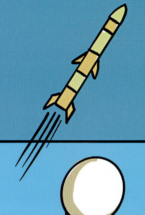

Average temperature: about 32 °F (0 °C)

Average temperature: up to 28 °F (-2 °C)

STRATOSPHERE

Average temperature: about -67 °F (-55 °C)

Average temperature: about -60 °F (-51 °C) at 6 miles (10 kilometers)

TROPOSPHERE

The lowest layer, the **troposphere,** is where nearly all of Earth's weather happens. Around 80 percent of the atmosphere's mass is in the troposphere. Gases in the troposphere trap some of the sun's heat, keeping Earth warm.

Average temperature: about 59 °F (15 °C)

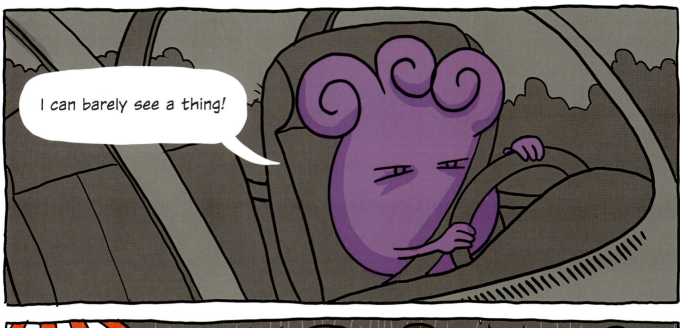

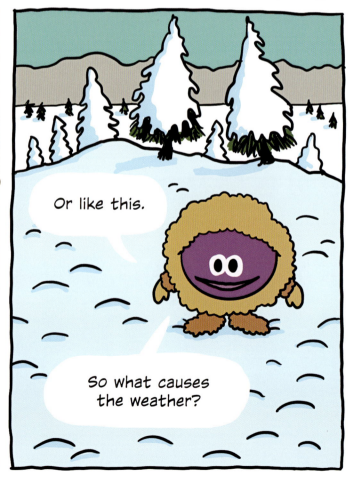

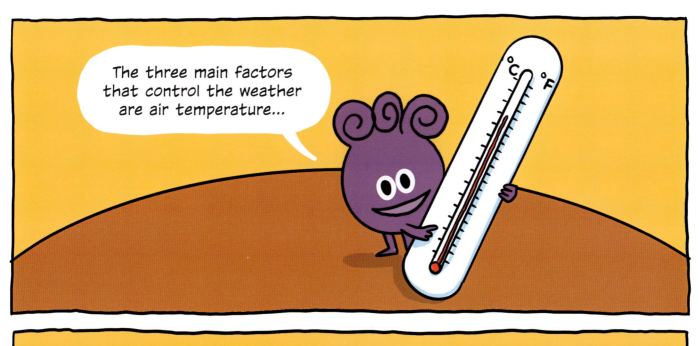

AIR TEMPERATURE

Phew! It's hot today! Why does the air temperature change? My friend Heat is here to help explain.

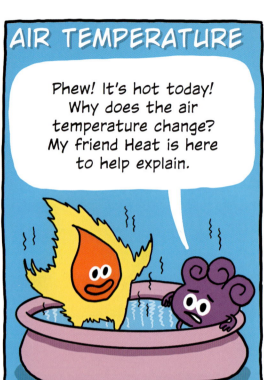

The air is warmed by radiation arriving from the sun. About 15 percent of the sun's radiation flows back into space, cooling the Earth.

The rest is trapped by gases in the atmosphere and warms Earth. This is called the *greenhouse effect* because the air acts like glass in a greenhouse!

Without the greenhouse effect, the air near Earth's surface would be about 59 °F (33 °C) cooler than it is.

Air temperature also depends on whether it's day or night. The sun's radiation only reaches Earth during daylight hours, so it's colder at night.

And it depends on your **altitude**. Within the troposphere, air temperature drops as you go higher.

Temperature also depends on the season. In winter, the sun is low in the sky and less of its radiation reaches Earth. Days are also shorter, which means fewer hours of sunshine.

The sun's radiation is one way to warm the air. Another way is through **conduction**. To understand that, we first need to learn something about me!

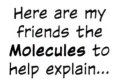

Here are my friends the **Molecules** to help explain...

Heat is a form of energy caused by the motion of molecules (us!) in a substance. If we're not moving around much, the substance will be cold.

But if we jiggle around fast, the substance will be hot. The faster we jiggle around, the hotter the substance is.

Conduction happens when we bump into each other. This causes heat energy to be transmitted through a substance.

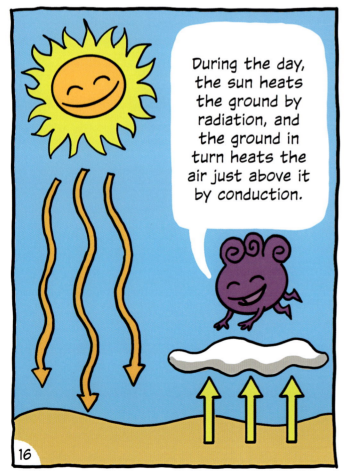

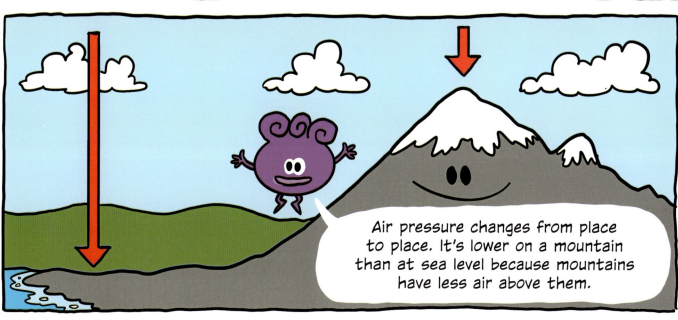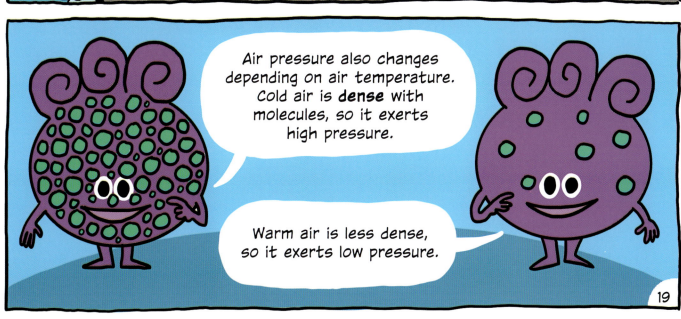

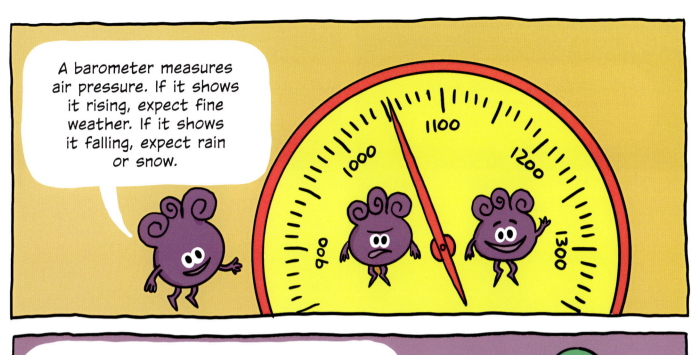

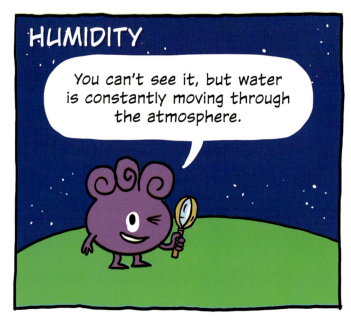
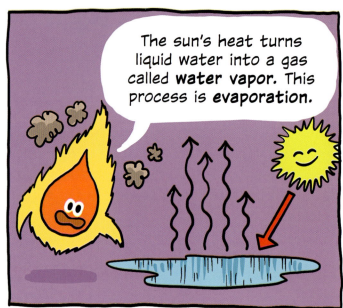

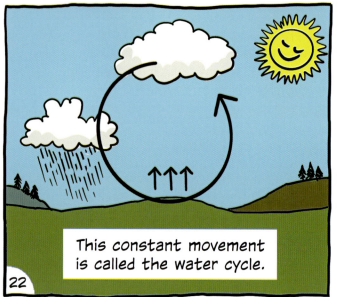
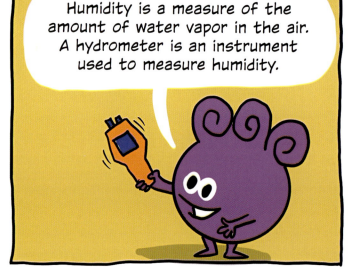

Weather reports often mention relative humidity (RH). This measures how close the air is to being saturated. RH is expressed as a percentage.

So if RH is 100 percent, the air is fully saturated, and the water vapor starts to condense into tiny droplets of water.

When this happens on the ground, we call it fog. If it happens in the sky, we call it a cloud.

Warm air can hold more water vapor than cold air. It takes much less water vapor for cold air to become saturated.

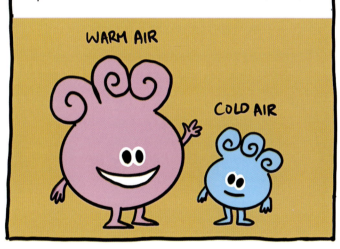

On some mornings, you might see dew—tiny drops of water that form on cool surfaces in the night. This happens because the air has been cooled in the night to the point of saturation.

If the temperature falls below freezing, small, white, icy crystals form. This is frost.

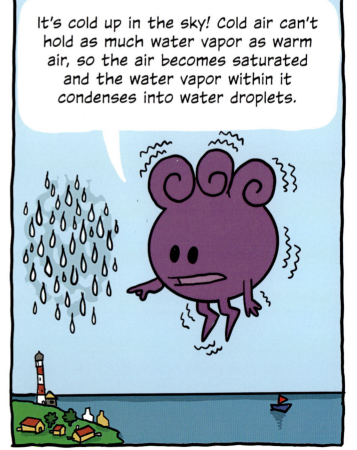

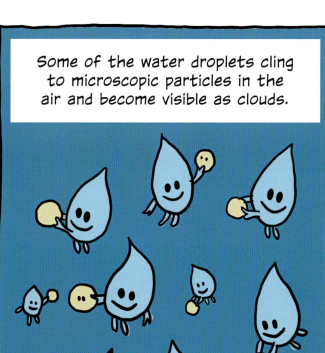

Some of the water droplets cling to microscopic particles in the air and become visible as clouds.

Stratus clouds appear as layers or sheets. These are the low-altitude gray or white clouds you often see on dull, overcast days.

Cumulus clouds appear as rounded masses, piled up on each other. They often remind me of cauliflowers or mashed potato. Yum!

Cirrus clouds are wispy clouds that appear at high altitudes and are formed from ice crystals, not water droplets. They remind me of tufts of hair. How do I look?

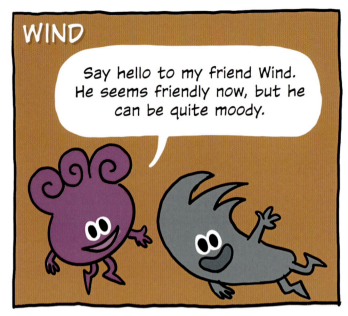

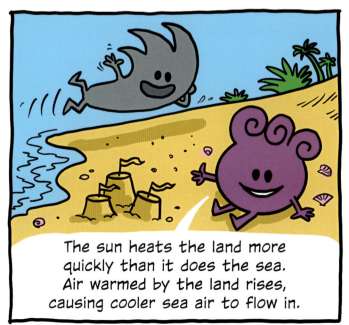
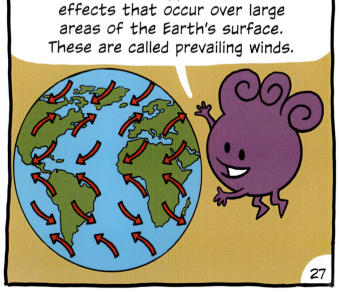

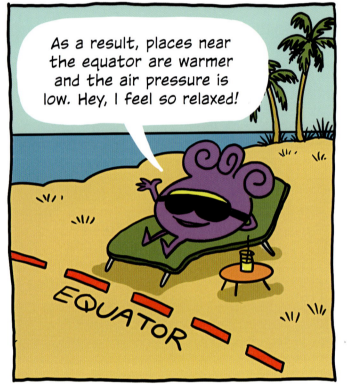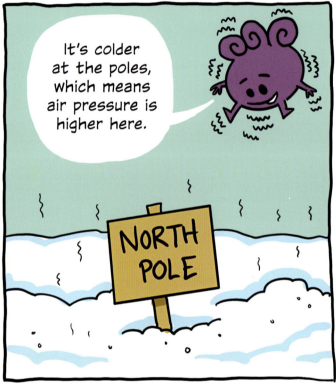

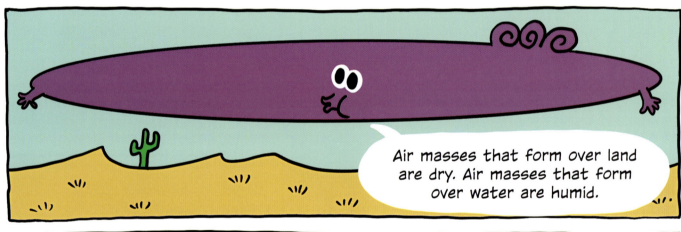

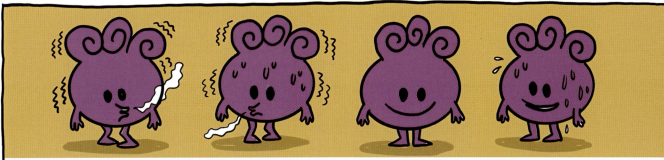

The four basic types of air mass are cold and dry, cold and humid, warm and dry, and warm and humid.

When winds move air masses, the air masses carry their weather with them. Hello, warm, dry land! I'm cold and wet!

As an air mass moves, its temperature and humidity can change as it moves over land or water. Hey, I'm feeling warmer and drier!

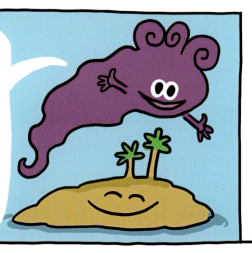

If a warm, humid air mass is forced up a mountain, its temperature drops and the relative humidity rises, leading to rain. Sorry! Blame the mountain!

FRONTS

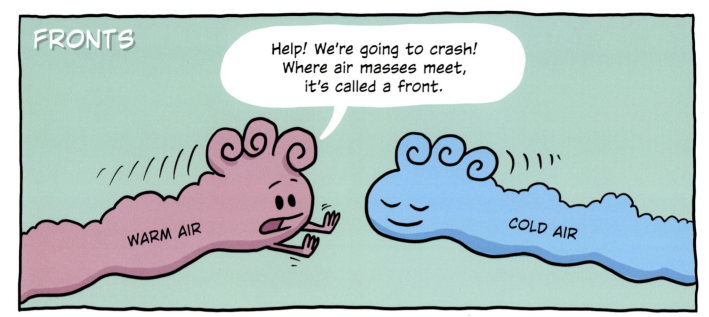

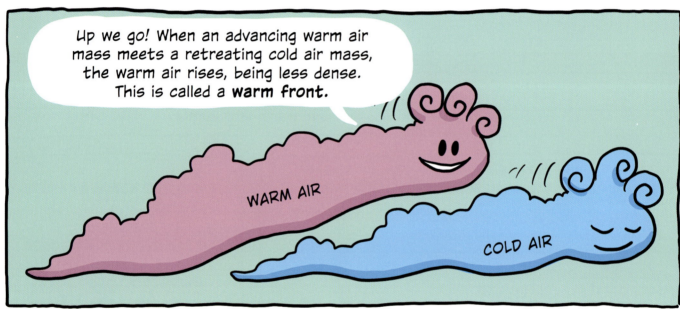

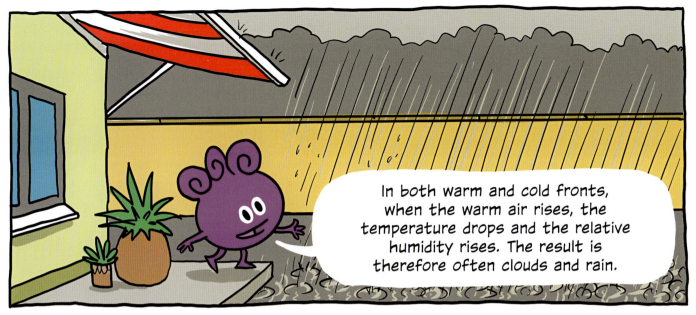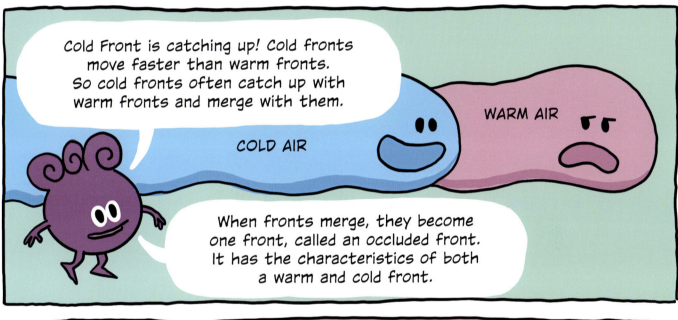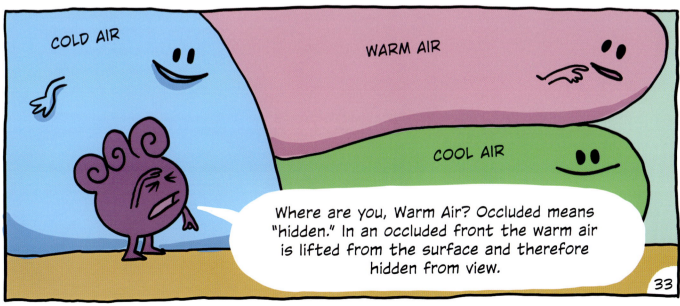

EXTREME WEATHER

LOOKING AFTER THE ATMOSPHERE

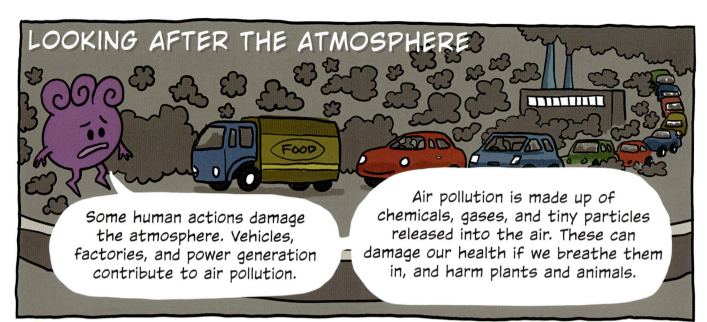

Some human actions damage the atmosphere. Vehicles, factories, and power generation contribute to air pollution.

Air pollution is made up of chemicals, gases, and tiny particles released into the air. These can damage our health if we breathe them in, and harm plants and animals.

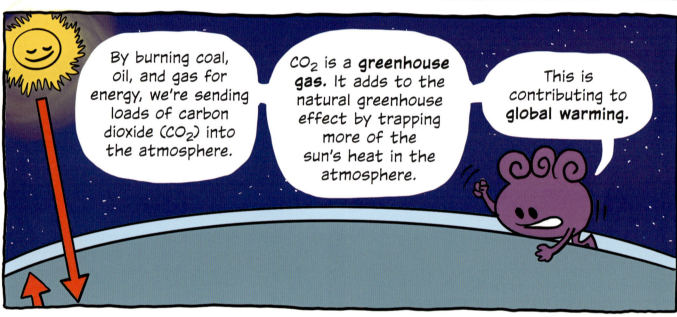

By burning coal, oil, and gas for energy, we're sending loads of carbon dioxide (CO_2) into the atmosphere.

CO_2 is a **greenhouse gas**. It adds to the natural greenhouse effect by trapping more of the sun's heat in the atmosphere.

This is contributing to **global warming**.

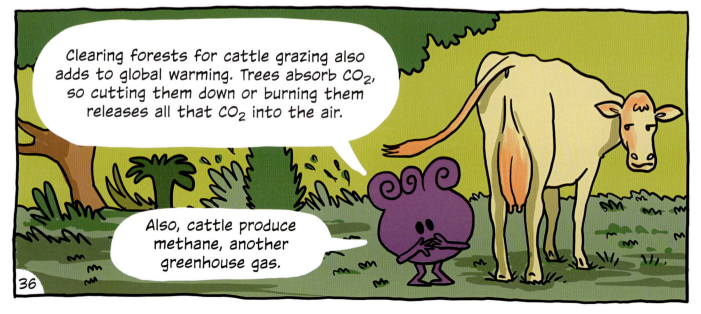

Clearing forests for cattle grazing also adds to global warming. Trees absorb CO_2, so cutting them down or burning them releases all that CO_2 into the air.

Also, cattle produce methane, another greenhouse gas.

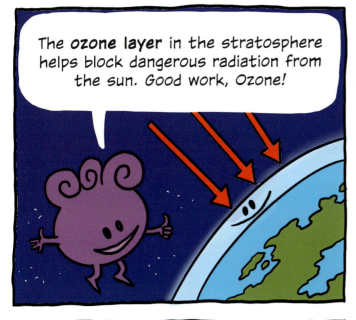
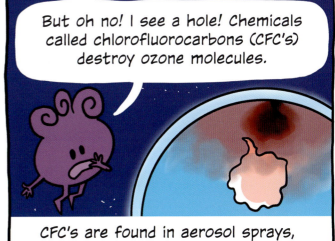

ACTIVITY: WEATHER OR NOT!

All the weather forecasters on television or radio have an annoying habit of talking about the weather without saying exactly what it is! See if you can give the correct term for the weather condition or event that they describe.

1. "These will make for a dull, overcast day all around!" _____

2. "The weather tonight will be dominated by air movement that is caused by air moving from areas of high to low pressure." _____

3. "We'll be surrounded for a few days with lighter air that rises." _____

4. "Residents will need to evacuate due to a storm with extremely high winds developing offshore, over the warm tropical ocean." _____

5. "These wispy clouds signal a change in the weather is coming!" _____

6. "Get ready for a weekend of high winds and heavy, blowing snow." _____

Word choices:

High pressure   Cirrus clouds   Hurricane
Blizzard   Front   Cumulus clouds
Humidity   Stratus clouds   Tornado
Low pressure   Wind   Temperature

See page 40 for answers.

7. "A great deal of water vapor in the air will make it feel sticky outside."

_____

8. "The sky will be filled with these fluffy masses as we enjoy pleasant weather the next few days!"

_____

9. "A whirling funnel of air is expected to form between the bottom of a storm cloud and the ground."

_____

10. "Atmosphere conditions will bring dry, sunny, settled weather for the next several days."

_____

11. "This number will tell you if you need to wear a coat or not today!"

_____

12. "Hovering over our area is this boundary between two air masses of different composition."

_____

WORDS TO KNOW

air mass a large body of air with about the same temperature, humidity, and pressure throughout.

air pressure the weight of air pressing down on Earth.

altitude the height of an object above Earth's surface.

cold front the boundary where an advancing cold air mass meets a retreating warm air mass.

conduction the process by which heat energy is transmitted through the collision of molecules within a substance.

convection the process by which heat energy is transmitted through the movement of molecules through a substance.

Coriolis effect an effect caused by the rotation of Earth, deflecting winds and causing them to move in a curve.

dense tightly packed.

evaporation the process by which a liquid turns into vapor.

global warming a gradual increase in the overall temperature of Earth's atmosphere.

greenhouse gas any gas that contributes to the greenhouse effect by trapping more of the sun's heat in the atmosphere.

mesosphere the region of Earth's atmosphere above the stratosphere and below the thermosphere.

molecule one of the basic units that make up matter.

ozone layer a layer in the stratosphere that contains a high concentration of the gas ozone.

radiation energy that travels from a heat source in the form of waves or energized particles.

saturation a state in which something is so soaked with water that no more can be absorbed.

stratosphere the region of Earth's atmosphere above the troposphere and below the mesosphere.

thermosphere the topmost layer of the atmosphere.

troposphere the lowest layer of the atmosphere.

warm front the boundary where an advancing warm air mass meets a retreating cold air mass.

water vapor water in the form of tiny droplets suspended in the air.

ACTIVITY ANSWERS 1. Stratus clouds; 2. Wind; 3. Low pressure; 4. Hurricane; 5. Cirrus clouds; 6. Blizzard; 7. Humidity; 8. Cumulus clouds; 9. Tornado; 10. High pressure; 11. Temperature; 12. Front